Special tool makes it extra easy!

Angled-tip hook

Learn to Crochet

D1197053

LEISURE ARTS, INC. • Maumelle, Arkansas

EDITORIAL STAFF
Senior Product Director: Pam Stebbins
Creative Art Director: Katherine Laughlin
Technical Writer: Sarah J. Green
Technical Editors: Linda A. Daley, Cathy Hardy, and Lois J. Long
Editorial Writer: Susan Frantz Wiles
Art Category Manager: Lora Puls
Graphic Artist: Jessica Bramlett
Prepress Technician: Stephanie Johnson

BUSINESS STAFF
President and Chief Executive Officer: Fred F. Pruss
Senior Vice President of Operations: Jim Dittrich
Vice President of Retail Sales: Martha Adams
Chief Financial Officer: Tiffany P. Childers
Controller: Teresa Eby
Information Technology Director: Brian Roden
Director of E-Commerce: Mark Hawkins
Manager of E-Commerce: Robert Young

Quick Start Guide illustrations by Matt Beynon

ISBN-13/EAN: 978-1-4647-1684-3

Meet the Designer:

Cony Larsen

Cony Larsen of Highland, Utah, is a designer and author of crochet books and tools. "I find inspiration all around me: the children in my life, my garden, and of course my love of hand-loomed textiles and fibers," she says. "My passion for preserving the art of crochet for future generations is what fuels my creative drive."

Cony learned to crochet when she was 6 years old. "Other crafts have sparked an interest for me — scrapbooking, quilting, knitting — but I always come back to my first love, crochet!"

Describing her style as Boho Chic with a touch of traditional, Cony says she loves projects that can be finished in a day or two, such as collars, hats, head-wraps, and other accessories. For more about her designs, tools, and aid programs for her Guatemalan homeland, visit her website, conylarsenbooks.com.

Let's get hooked on crochet! Learning is simple with our step-by-step instructions and pictures. The special beginner's crochet hook that came with this book gives you an extra advantage; its angled tip is easier to insert into stitches. This is important because many beginners tend to make tight stitches and get frustrated with this step. Your special hook will let you breeze through the learning process and start making the fun designs we've included, from bows and flowers to a phone sleeve and cute bag. You'll love the creative world of crochet!

Quick Start Guide

Left hand is crucial It is important that you control your tension so it's **not too tight or too loose**, but just right! Just like a sewing machine has knobs to control the thread tension, your left hand's **pinky and ring fingers are crucial** to control the tension and feed the yarn smoothly to the hook!

Too loose This is how it works, if you hold the yarn too loose, your stitches will be "loopy" and big and it will be confusing to see where the next stitch should be worked. The result will be a bigger gauge or fit.

Or, too tight If you hold your yarn too tight, your stitches will be small and tight, sometimes so tight that you won't be able to put your hook through the next stitch! The result will be a tighter gauge or fit.

To achieve the right tension or gauge, you must start with the yarn and hook size specified in the pattern; you can choose a different yarn as long as it's the same weight that your pattern requires. Read what the Gauge is supposed to be for the pattern. Our patterns will specify how many stitches or rows you should get per inch.

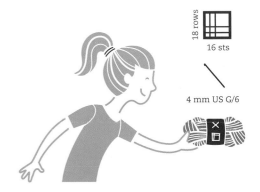

18 rows

16 sts

4 mm US G/6

Crochet a swatch with the basic stitch specified in the pattern, usually a 2" x 2" or 4" x 4" swatch made of single crochets. Measure how many stitches "fit" in one inch. In the sample above, 4 stitches equal approximately 1".

Measuring Checking the Gauge is simply measuring the number of stitches and rows per inch of crocheting. Gauge is usually tested on a single crochet swatch. Place a ruler or a measuring tape across the center of a swatch to see how many stitches "fit" in one inch. Do the same with the rows. In the swatch above, 5 rows equal approximately 1".

A Grid Some yarns have the gauge on the packaging; for example, you might see a grid with a 16 on one side and an 18 on the other side and a hook with a number on it. This is very helpful as it tells you that the average crocheter using the hook size that they specified will crochet a swatch measuring the same as the grid on the label.

Oh no! My gauge is not correct, what can I do?
Try one or all of these 3 solutions to correct your gauge:
1. Try changing hook sizes, either a bigger hook for bigger stitches or a smaller hook for smaller stitches. **2. You may change your yarn size** and brand. **3. Hold your yarn tighter or loosen your grip** on the yarn to adjust the tension; see first illustration on page 4. Check your gauge periodically to make sure your garment will be the right size when you're finished.

Why check gauge?
Many crocheters think that working a swatch is a waste of time, however, you don't want to work forty hours on a garment that won't fit — that would be a bigger waste of time!
Remember, change the hook, change the yarn, adjust the tension, and try again!

Let's Get Started!

Even if you are eager to start on your favorite project in this book, it is important that you follow the lessons in the order given. Each will build your skills by introducing a stitch or technique and then providing a project using those new skills.

The special crochet hook that came with this book was especially designed for beginners. It has an angled point that allows it to slip easily into the stitches. (After you work with this hook a little while, you'll be ready to move on to standard crochet hooks.)

A good yarn to use with your special hook is a light weight yarn. Look for a yarn that has an icon on it like this ⬛ on the yarn label. Choose a bright color of yarn because it will make it easier for you to see the stitches you make.

Begin by learning the right way of Holding Your Hook and Holding the Yarn and you will be on your way!

Holding Your Hook

The best way to hold a hook is like a pencil, with the hook tip facing you!

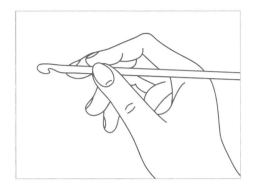

1: Place your thumb on the grip "flat" section of the hook.

2: Your index finger should be on the opposite side of the "flat" section of the hook.

3: Your middle finger should be about 1" (2.5 cm) from the tip; this gives you more control and freedom of movement.

In regards to movement, the secret is in your wrist! The hook doesn't move, let the wrist do all the work. Let your wrist bend and twist as needed. Your hook remains in the same steady grip.

Holding the Yarn

This is the right way to hold the yarn.

1: With your index finger, hold the yarn up. This finger serves as the "feeding" finger; it feeds more yarn to your hook.

2: Use your pinky and ring fingers to hold the yarn against the palm of your hand; this is how you control the tension. Pinch the yarn against the palm of your hand softly to control your tension. If you pinch too soft, your stitches will be big and loopy. If you pinch too hard, your stitches will be tight and it will be difficult to insert your hook in the next stitch; try to pinch it just right.

3: Your middle finger and thumb serve to steady your project close to the hook. Make sure to always "pinch" your project right up to the area where the hook is. Why? This will give you more control when inserting the hook in the next stitch.

Slip Knot

To make a slip knot, pull a length of yarn from the skein. Make a circle on top of the yarn that comes from the skein about 6" (15 cm) from the end.

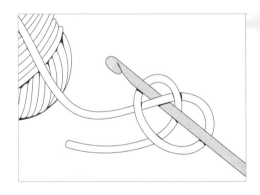

Slip your hook under the strand in the middle of the circle. Pull on both strands to tighten the slip knot.

The great thing about the slip knot is that it's easy to adjust and also to un-do. To practice, just slip the hook out of the loop and pull on both ends of the yarn until the slip knot disappears!

Chain (ch)

Step 1: Start with a slip knot on your hook.

Step 2: Yarn over (yo) the hook...

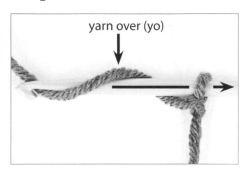

yarn over (yo)

Step 3: Pull yarn through the loop on your hook, chain (ch) completed.

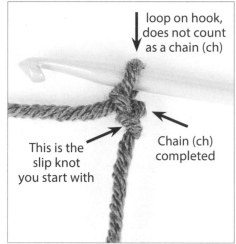

loop on hook, does not count as a chain (ch)

This is the slip knot you start with

Chain (ch) completed

Step 4: Yarn over (yo) again, repeat Step 3, second chain (ch) completed. Now, practice making 200 chains. Make sure they are not "loopy" or too tight; try to make them just right! If you make them too loopy, it will be hard to define where to insert the hook next. If you make the chains too tight, it will be hard to insert the hook in the next loop.

yarn over (yo) again

About your Chains (chs): Stop for a minute to look at your chains (chs). They look like little hearts strung together. Also, notice the loop on your hook is not a chain (ch); it is just the loop on your hook, don't count it as a chain (ch).

Practice, practice, practice; then go to the Chain, Chain, Chain Necklace project on page 8.

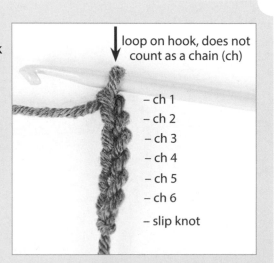

loop on hook, does not count as a chain (ch)

– ch 1
– ch 2
– ch 3
– ch 4
– ch 5
– ch 6

– slip knot

Chain, Chain, Chain Necklace

This is the perfect beginner's first project. You will love the simplicity of it.
You can choose wood beads or buttons to decorate it, or just finish it with a tassel!

 BEGINNER

Finished Size: Approximately 28" (71 cm) in circumference

SHOPPING LIST

Yarn (Fine Weight)

[.35 ounces, 38.3 yards
(10 grams, 35 meters) per ball]:

☐ 1 Ball **each** red, orange, yellow,
green, turquoise, and white

Crochet Hook

☐ Size E (3.5 mm)
or size needed for gauge

Additional Supplies

☐ Yarn needle
☐ Decorative wood beads
(optional)

GAUGE INFORMATION

6 chains = 1" (2.5 cm)

Gauge is not essential for this project; however, you do need to stay within the number of chains per inch indicated above for your Chain Necklace to have the same finished size as our sample. See illustration below for actual size of chains and measure your chains against our swatch to see if you are staying within the gauge specified. You may use any cotton yarn that will yield the gauge needed.

This is actual size of chains
6 Chains = 1"

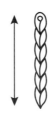

INSTRUCTIONS

Skills Learned: With this project you will practice making **chains (chs)** until they become so easy to make that you can do it with your eyes closed! Go ahead, try it with your eyes closed and see how good you are at working them. You will also learn to make **The Perfect Tassel** with instructions on page 45.

Chain Necklace

Make 6 chains, one in each color: red, orange, yellow, green, turquoise, and white.

Try to maintain a consistent tension to make each chain the same size. They should look like small beads, not "loopy" or big, you should not be able to see any light coming through the loops when you hold it up, and they should not be so tight that you can't pull your hook out of the loops.

Row 1: Ch 200. Fasten off leaving a 6" (15 cm) tail; you will use this tail to thread through the beads.

Beading Technique

Hold one of the 6" (15 cm) tails from one of the strands and thread it through one of the beads, repeat with all six strands; move bead down to mark the center of the necklace.

*Separate strands into groups of 3, **slip each group of 3 into a bead and move bead down about 3½" (9 cm) from center bead; rep from ** for the other group of 3 strands; hold the 6" (15 cm) tails again and thread all 6 strands into one bead; rep from ** again. Repeat from * to ** to work the other side of necklace. Gather all strands together at the end, cut a piece of the cotton yarn about 16" (40.5 cm) long and fold in half, wrap around all the strands tightly and fasten with a knot, trim all thread knot ends under wraps.

Tassel

Make tassel following instructions on page 45, and tie around front bead.

9

Single Crochet (sc)

Row 1 - Step 1: Work 11 chains (chs); see instructions on page 7. Remember, the loop on the hook does not count as a chain (ch). You will work the first Single Crochet (sc) in the second chain (ch) from the hook; you skip ch 1 because it is used as a height allowance (to raise the yarn to the height of a single crochet). Let's count the chains (chs).

loop on hook, does not count as a chain (ch)

ch 1
ch 2
ch 3
ch 4
ch 5
ch 6
ch 7
ch 8
ch 9
ch 10
ch 11
slip knot

Step 2: Insert hook in 2nd chain (ch) from hook (or specified stitch), yarn over (yo).

Step 3: Pull yarn through chain (ch) (or specified stitch). You should have two loops on your hook.

Step 4: Yarn over (yo) and pull yarn through both loops on hook.

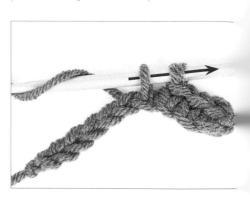

Completed Single Crochet (sc):

Work the next single crochet (sc) in the next chain (ch) and in each remaining chain (ch); following Steps 2 through 4. You should have 10 single crochets (scs) total.

How To Turn At The End Of A Row

Let's take a minute to study what your single crochets (scs) look like. This is how the front side of your single crochets (scs) look; notice the front and back loops at the top of each single crochet (sc).

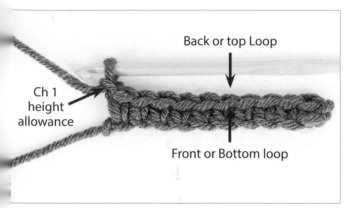

Back Loop - Front Loop

If you work your next row by inserting the hook in the back loop only, you will get a different textured fabric than if you insert the hook in the front loop only! You will have a chance to practice this simple "back loop/front loop" technique on one of our projects ahead!

Let's continue...after you complete the last single crochet (sc), you will need to turn, right? To turn, work 1 chain (ch) for a height allowance.

Row 2: Turn your work so the back of the first row is now facing you.

This is how the back side of your single crochets (scs) look; you can see a small horizontal bar at the top of each sc rather than a front and a back loop.

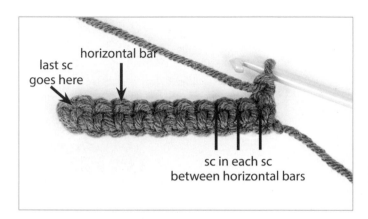

Work Row 2 as follows, insert your hook under both top loops of 1st single crochet (sc) (between the small horizontal bars), yarn over (yo), work Steps 3 and 4 to complete your first single crochet (sc). Work next single crochet (sc) in the next single crochet (sc) and in each remaining single crochet (sc) following Steps 2 through 4. Don't overlook the last single crochet (sc); the insert place is not as defined as prior stitches. Make sure to count your stitches if you are not sure you worked the last single crochet (sc) of this row. You should have 10 single crochets (scs) total; chain (ch) 1, and turn.

Rows 3-8: Repeat Row 2, work 1 chain (ch) for height allowance at the end of each row. When you get to the end of Row 8, work a chain (ch), cut yarn leaving a 4" (10 cm) tail. To fasten off, see next step.

Fasten Off: Pull the 4" (10 cm) tail with your hook through the last chain (ch), pull the tail to tighten the last chain (ch) made and to secure the last stitch so it doesn't unravel.

How To Count Rows

Counting rows can be difficult sometimes; you will need to be familiar with how each row looks on the front and back sides. For quick reference, the front of a single crochet has two little vertical legs and the back has a little horizontal bar. Your swatch should have 8 rows, see photo.

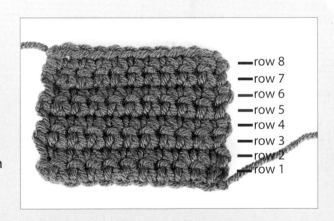

—row 8
—row 7
—row 6
—row 5
—row 4
—row 3
—row 2
—row 1

Practice, practice, practice; then go to the Bows on Clips project.

Bows on Clips

BEGINNER

Finished Sizes: **Small bow** is 3¾" x 2" (9.5 cm x 5 cm). **Medium bow** is 5" x 2¾" (12.5 cm x 7 cm).
Large bow is 6" x 3" (15 cm x 7.5 cm).

SHOPPING LIST

Yarn (Light Weight)
[3.5 ounces, 218 yards
(100 grams, 199 meters) per skein]:

Small Bow

☐ Blue - 1 skein

Large Bow (pg. 23)

☐ Coral - 1 skein

☐ Cream - 1 skein

Crochet Hook

☐ Size E (3.5 mm)

or size needed for gauge

Additional Supplies

☐ Tapestry needle

☐ 1" (2.5 cm) wide Headband - 2

OR

☐ 2" (5 cm) Hair clip - 2

GAUGE INFORMATION

6 sts = 1" (2.5 cm), 6 rows =1" (2.5 cm)

Gauge is not essential for this project.
You may use thinner yarn or crochet
cotton for smaller bows, or chunky yarn
for bigger bows. Make sure to change
your hook size accordingly. You may
use any cotton yarn that will yield the
gauge.

Rows 3-44: Rep Row 2. Fasten off leaving a 12" (30.5 cm) tail; thread tail through a tapestry needle, stitch ends of bow together with whipstitch. Move seam to the center back of bow and pinch together at the center, wrap remaining tail around the center and fasten off. Weave in ends.

Strap

Ch 5.

Row 1: Sc in 2nd ch from hook, sc in next 3 chs; ch 1, turn, (4 scs).

Rows 2-9: Sc in each sc across; ch 1, turn.

Fasten off leaving a 12" (30.5 cm) tail; thread tail through a tapestry needle, wrap Strap around center of Bow, stitch Strap's ends together with whipstitch. Weave in ends.

Finishing

Secure Small Bow to a headband with hot glue or stitch to metal hair clip.

INSTRUCTIONS
Small Bow

Skills Learned: This will help you to practice your **Single Crochets** (scs); you will also learn a new technique, working on the **Back Loop Only** (BLO) of scs.

Ch 13.

Row 1: Sc in 2nd ch from hook, sc in each ch across; ch 1, turn, (12 scs).

Row 2: Sc in 1st sc, sc in BLO (Back Loop Only) of next 10 sc, sc in last sc; ch 1, turn, (12 scs).

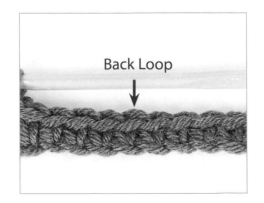

Back Loop

Medium Bow

Skills Learned: This will help you to practice your **Single Crochets** (scs); you will also learn a new technique, working **Through Center of Core** (TCC) of scs.

Ch 14.

Row 1: Sc in 2nd ch from hook, sc in each ch across; ch 1, turn, (13 scs).

Row 2: Sc in 1st sc, sc TCC (Through Center of Core) of next 11 sc, sc in last sc; ch 1, turn, (13 scs).

center of core

Rows 3-58: Rep Row 2 until bow measures 9" (23 cm) long, (13 scs).

Fasten off leaving a 12" (30.5 cm) tail; thread tail through a tapestry needle, stitch ends of bow together with whipstitch. Move seam to the center back of bow and pinch together at the center, wrap remaining tail around the center and fasten off.

Weave in ends.

Strap

Ch 6.

Row 1: Sc in 2nd ch from hook, sc in next 4 chs; ch 1, turn, (5 scs).

Rows 2-12: Sc in each sc across; ch 1, turn.

Fasten off leaving a 12" (30.5 cm) tail; thread tail through a tapestry needle, wrap Strap around center of Bow, stitch Strap's ends together with whipstitch. Weave in ends.

Finishing

Secure Medium Bow to a headband with hot glue or stitch to metal hair clip.

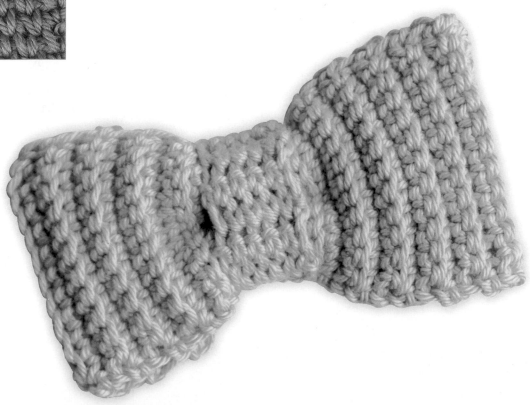

Slip Stitch (sl st)

Row 1 - Step 1: Work 11 chains (chs); see instructions on page 7. Remember, the loop on the hook does not count as a chain (ch). You will work the first Slip Stitch (sl st) in the second chain (ch) from the hook; you skip ch 1 because it is used as a height allowance (to raise the yarn to the height of a Slip Stitch. Let's count the chains (chs).

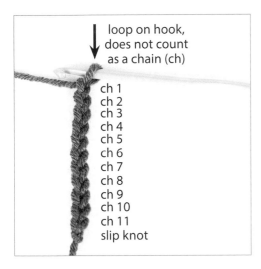

Step 2: Insert hook in 2ⁿᵈ chain (ch) from hook (or specified stitch), yarn over (yo).

Step 3: Pull yarn through chain (ch) (or specified stitch) and through the loop on your hook.

Completed Slip Stitch (sl st): Work next slip stitch (sl st) in the next chain (ch) and in each remaining chain (ch) following Steps 2 through 3. You should have 10 slip stitches (sl sts) total.

How To Turn At The End Of A Row

Let's take a minute to study how your slip stitches (sl sts) look. This is how the front side of your slip stitches (sl sts) look; notice the front and back loops at the top of your row and how the stitches look interlocked. Slip Stitches (sl sts) make a very dense fabric because the stitches are very short. Let's continue... after you complete the last slip stitch (sl st), you will need to turn, right? To turn, work 1 chain (ch) for height allowance.

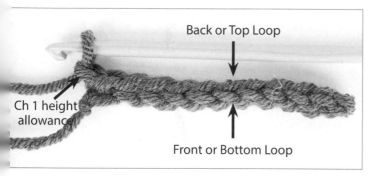

Ch 1 height allowance

Back or Top Loop

Front or Bottom Loop

Row 2:
Turn your work so the back of the first row is now facing you.

Work Row 2 as follows, work in the front loop of each slip stitch (sl st), repeat Steps 2 and 3 to complete second row. Don't overlook the first and last slip stitch (sl st); the insert place is not as defined as prior stitches. Make sure to count your stitches if you are not sure you worked the last slip stitch (sl st) of this row. You should have 10 slip stitches (sl sts) total; chain (ch) 1, and turn.

Rows 3-10:
Repeat Row 2, work 1 chain (ch) for height allowance at the end of each row. When you get to the end of Row 10, work a chain (ch), cut yarn leaving a 4" (10 cm) tail to fasten off.

Fasten Off:
Pull the tail with your hook through the last chain (ch), pull the tail to tighten the last chain (ch) and to secure the last stitch (st) so it doesn't unravel.

How To Count Rows

Counting rows can be difficult sometimes. You will need to be familiar with how each row looks on the front and back sides. For quick reference, the front of a slip stitch (sl st) looks like interlocking little bars; the back of a slip stitch (sl st) looks like attached little dash lines. Each row has a front and a back loop at the top of the row; work on the front loop each time.

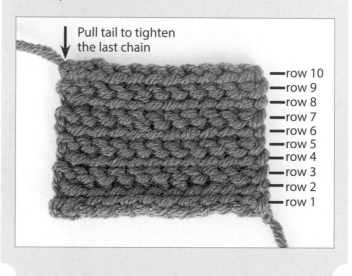

Pull tail to tighten the last chain

row 10
row 9
row 8
row 7
row 6
row 5
row 4
row 3
row 2
row 1

Circle Me Pretty Necklace

Circles are very versatile, meaning they can work for a variety of projects. Use circles to make the top of a hat, make flowers, necklaces, join them to make a fun blanket or a headband. Your imagination is the limit!

⬤▭▭▭ **BEGINNER**

Finished Size: See sizes with each circle pattern.

SHOPPING LIST

Yarn (Fine Weight)

[.35 ounces, 38.3 yards (10 grams, 35 meters) per ball]:
- ☐ 1 ball **each** orange, yellow, and turquoise

Crochet Hook
- ☐ Size E (3.5 mm) **or** size needed for gauge

Additional Supplies
- ☐ Tapestry needle
- ☐ Tiny wood beads or brads for Circles' center
- ☐ Chain or leather string for necklace

GAUGE INFORMATION

Gauge is not essential for this project.

INSTRUCTIONS

Skills Learned: With this project you will learn to work in circles starting with a **Magic Ring** (see pg. 44). You will also practice making **single crochets (scs)**.

Small Circle

make 2 of the same color
approximately 1¾" (4.5 cm) across

Make a Magic Ring.

Rnd 1: Ch 1, work 8 sc in ring. Join with sl st to beg sc, (8 sts).

Rnd 2: Ch 1, 2 sc in each sc. Join with sl st to beg sc, (16 sts).

Rnd 3: Ch 1, sc in each sc. Join with sl st to beg sc, (16 sts).

Rnd 4: Ch 1, sc in 1st sc, *2 sc in next sc, sc in next sc; rep from * around. Join with sl st to beg sc, (24 sts).

Rnds 5-6: Rep Rnd 3 until circle measures approximately 1¾" (4.5 cm) across. Join with sl st to beg sc.

Edging (optional)

Rnd 1: Sl st in 1st sc, *ch 1, sl st in next sc; rep from * across. Join with sl st to beg sl st. Fasten off. Weave in ends.

Medium Circle

approximately 2" (5 cm) across

Make a Magic Ring.

Rnd 1: Ch 1, work 8 sc in ring. Join with sl st to beg sc, (8 sts).

Rnd 2: Ch 1, 2 sc in each sc. Join with sl st to beg sc, (16 sts).

Rnd 3: Ch 1, sc in each sc. Join with sl st to beg sc, (16 sts).

Rnd 4: Ch 1, sc in 1st sc, *2 sc in next sc, sc in next sc; rep from * around. Join with sl st to beg sc, (24 sts).

Rnd 5: Ch 1, sc in 1st sc, *2 sc in next sc, sc in next 2 sc; rep from * around. Join with sl st to beg sc, (32 sts).

Rnds 6-7: Rep Rnd 3 until circle measures approximately 2" (5 cm) across.

Work optional Edging instructions.

Large Circle

approximately 2¾" (7 cm) across

Make a Magic Ring.

Rnd 1: Ch 1, work 8 sc in ring. Join with sl st to beg sc, (8 sts).

Rnd 2: Ch 1, 2 sc in each sc. Join with sl st to beg sc, (16 sts).

Rnd 3: Ch 1, sc in each sc. Join with sl st to beg sc, (16 sts).

Rnd 4: Ch 1, sc in 1st sc, *2 sc in next sc, sc in next sc; rep from * around. Join with sl st to beg sc, (24 sts).

Rnd 5: Ch 1, sc in 1st sc, *2 sc in next sc, sc in next 2 sc; rep from * around. Join with sl st to beg sc, (32 sts).

Rnd 6: Ch 1, sc in 1st sc, *2 sc in next sc, sc in next 3 sc; rep from * around. Join with sl st to beg sc, (40 sts).

Rnds 7-8: Rep Rnd 3 until circle measures approximately 2¾" (7 cm) across.

Work optional Edging instructions.

Finishing

Stack circles with smallest circle on top; secure all circles together with a brad through the centers, or a button, and make sure you sew through all layers.

Take second Small Circle and cover back of flower; thread a yarn needle with matching yarn, attach in place with whipstitch.

Run chain through back of Circles to make necklace (see photo below).

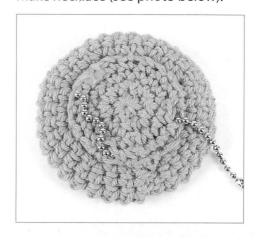

Half Double Crochet (hdc)

Row 1 - Step 1: Work 12 chains (chs), see instructions on page 7; remember, the loop on the hook does not count as a chain (ch). You will work the first Half Double Crochet (hdc) in the 3rd chain (ch) from the hook; you skip chains 1 and 2 because they are used as a height allowance (to raise the yarn to the height of a half double crochet). Let's count the chains (chs).

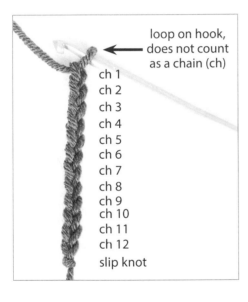

loop on hook, does not count as a chain (ch)

ch 1
ch 2
ch 3
ch 4
ch 5
ch 6
ch 7
ch 8
ch 9
ch 10
ch 11
ch 12
slip knot

Step 2: Yarn over (yo), insert hook in 3rd chain (ch) from hook (or specified stitch).

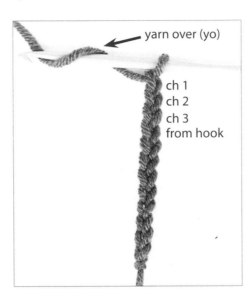

yarn over (yo)

ch 1
ch 2
ch 3
from hook

Step 3: Yarn over (yo) and pull yarn through chain (ch) (or specified stitch). You should have 3 loops on your hook...

Step 4: Yarn over (yo) and pull yarn through all loops on hook.

Completed Half Double Crochet (hdc) Work next half double crochet (hdc) in the next chain (ch) and in each remaining chain (ch) following Steps 2 through 4. You should have 10 half double crochets (hdcs) total.

How To Turn At The End Of A Row

Let's take a minute to study how your half double crochets (hdcs) look. This is how the front side of your half double crochets (hdcs) look; notice the two little vertical legs with a diagonal horizontal bar on top of the little legs. Let's continue...after you complete the last half double crochet (hdc), you will need to turn, right? To turn, work 2 chains (chs) for the height allowance...

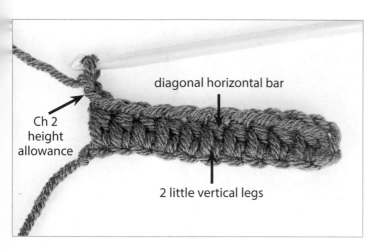

Ch 2 height allowance

diagonal horizontal bar

2 little vertical legs

Row 2: Turn your work so the back of the first row is now facing you. This is how the back of your hdcs look; you can see a bottom loop and a top loop with a hole in the center.

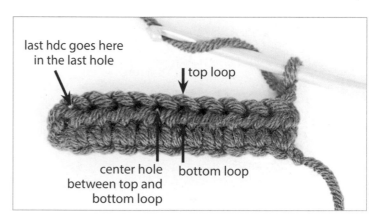

last hdc goes here in the last hole

top loop

center hole between top and bottom loop

bottom loop

Work Row 2 as follows, yarn over (yo), insert your hook in the center hole between the top and bottom loops of 1st half double crochet (hdc), work Steps 3 and 4 to complete your first. Work next half double crochet (hdc) in the next half double crochet (hdc) and in each remaining half double crochet (hdc) following Steps 2 through 4. Don't overlook the last half double crochet (hdc); the insert place is not as defined as prior stitches. Make sure to count your stitches if you are not sure you worked the last half double crochet (hdc) of this row. You should have 10 half double crochets (hdcs) total; chain (ch) 2 for height allowance, and turn.

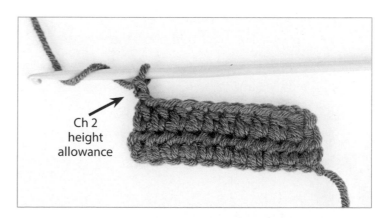

Ch 2 height allowance

Rows 3-6: Repeat Row 2, work 2 chains (chs) for height allowance at the end of each row.

Fasten Off: When you get to the end of Row 6, work a chain (ch), cut yarn leaving a 4" (10 cm) tail to fasten off. Pull the 4" (10 cm) tail with your hook through the last chain (ch), pull the tail to tighten the last chain (ch) made and to secure the last stitch so it doesn't unravel.

How To Count Rows

Counting rows can be difficult sometimes. You will need to be familiar with how each row looks on the front and back sides. Please note that half double crochets (hdcs) are a bit taller than single crochets (sc), so you work less rows for a project. For quick reference, the front of a half double crochet (hdc) has two little vertical legs with a diagonal horizontal bar across the top of the little legs and the back has a top and a bottom loop with a hole in between. Your swatch should have 6 rows, see swatch.

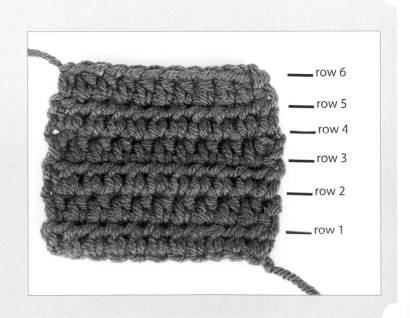

— row 6
— row 5
— row 4
— row 3
— row 2
— row 1

Large Bow

See page 13 for Shopping List.

Skills Learned: This will help you to practice your **Half Double Crochets** (hdcs).

Ch 14.

Row 1: Sc in 2nd ch from hook, sc in each ch across, ch 1, turn, (13 scs).

Row 2: Sc in 1st sc, hdc in next 11 scs, sc in last sc, ch 1, turn, (13 sts).

Row 3: Sc in 1st sc, hdc in next 11 hdcs, sc in last sc, ch 1, turn, (13 sts).

Rows 4-42: Rep Row 3 until bow measures 12" long, (13 sts).

Fasten off leaving a 12" (30.5 cm) tail; thread tail through a tapestry needle, stitch ends of bow together with whipstitch. Move seam to the center back of bow and pinch together at the center, wrap remaining tail around the center and fasten off. Weave in ends.

Strap
Ch 6.

Row 1: Sc in 2nd ch from hook, sc in next 4 chs, ch 1, turn, (5 scs).

Rows 2-15: Sc in each sc across, ch 1, turn.

Fasten off leaving a 12" (30.5 cm) tail; thread tail through a tapestry needle, wrap Strap around center of Bow, stitch Strap's ends together with whipstitch. Weave in ends.

Finishing
Secure Large Bow to a headband with hot glue or stitch to metal hair clip.

Double Crochet (dc)

Row 1 - Step 1: Work 13 chains (chs), see instructions on page 7; remember, the loop on the hook does not count as a chain (ch). You will work the first Double Crochet (dc) in the 4th chain (ch) from the hook; you skip ch 1, 2, and 3 because they are used as a height allowance (to raise the yarn to the height of a double crochet). Let's count the chains (chs).

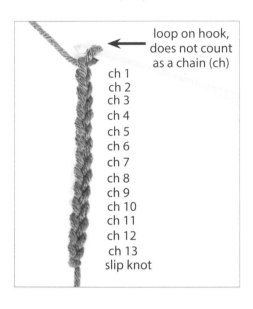

loop on hook, does not count as a chain (ch)

ch 1
ch 2
ch 3
ch 4
ch 5
ch 6
ch 7
ch 8
ch 9
ch 10
ch 11
ch 12
ch 13
slip knot

Step 2: Yarn over (yo).

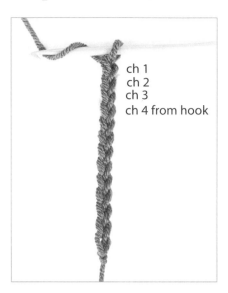

ch 1
ch 2
ch 3
ch 4 from hook

Step 3: Insert hook in 4th chain (ch) from hook (or specified stitch).

Step 4: Yarn over (yo) and pull yarn through chain (ch) (or specified stitch). You should have 3 loops on your hook...

Step 5: Yarn over (yo) and pull yarn through 2 loops on hook, you should have 2 loops left on your hook.

Step 6: Yarn over (yo) again and pull yarn through the last 2 loops on the hook.

How To Turn At The End Of A Row

Let's take a minute to study how your double crochets (dcs) look. This is how the front side of your double crochets (dcs) look; notice the two little vertical legs with 2 diagonal bars on top of the little legs. Let's continue.... after you complete the last double crochet (dc), you will need to turn, right? To turn, work 3 chains (chs) for height allowance because double crochets (dcs) are much taller than single crochets (scs) and half double crochets (hdcs).

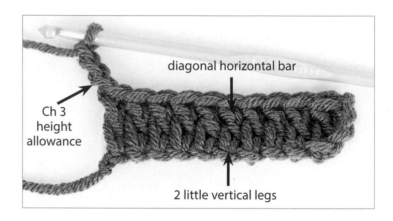

Ch 3 height allowance

diagonal horizontal bar

2 little vertical legs

Completed Double Crochet (dc)

And now do it again! Yarn over (yo), work next double crochet (dc) in the next chain (ch) and in each remaining chain (ch) following Steps 2 through 6. You should have 10 double crochets (dcs) total.

Row 2: Turn your work so the back of the first row is now facing you. This is how the back of your dcs look: you can see 2 horizontal bars on top of the body (which looks like a column of interlocking stitches) of each double crochet (dc).

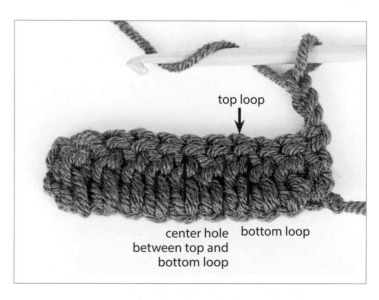

top loop

center hole between top and bottom loop

bottom loop

Work Row 2 as follows, Yarn over (yo), insert

your hook in the center hole between the two horizontal bars of 1st double crochet (dc), work Steps 4 through 6 to complete your first double crochet (dc). Work next double crochet (dc) in the next hole at the top of the next double crochet (dc) and in each remaining double crochet (dc) following Steps 2 through 6. Don't overlook the first and last double crochets (dcs); the insert place is not as defined as the stitches in between. Make sure to count your stitches if you are not sure you worked the last double crochet (dc) of this row. You should have a total of 10 double crochets (dcs), chain (ch) 3 and turn.

Fasten Off: When you get to the end of Row 4, work

a chain (ch), cut yarn leaving a 4" (10 cm) tail to fasten off; pull the 4" (10 cm) tail with your hook through the last chain (ch), pull the tail to tighten the last chain (ch) made and to secure the last stitch so it doesn't unravel.

last dc goes here in the last hole

Rows 3-4: Repeat Row 2, work 3 chains (chs) for

height allowance at the end of each row.

Ch 3 height allowance

How To Count Rows

Counting rows can be difficult sometimes. You will need to be familiar with how each row looks on the front and back sides. Please note that double crochets (dcs) are a bit taller than half double crochets (hdc), and are double the size of single crochets (scs), so you work less rows for a project.

For quick reference, the front of a double crochet (dc) has two little vertical legs with 2 diagonal bars across the top of the little legs and the back of a double crochet (dc) has 2 horizontal bars on top of the body (which looks like a column of interlocking stitches) of each double crochet (dc). Your swatch should have 4 rows, see swatch.

—— row 4
—— row 3
—— row 2
—— row 1

Flower Power

BEGINNER

Finished Size: See sizes with each flower pattern.

SHOPPING LIST

Yarn (Light Weight) [LIGHT 3]
[3.5 ounces, 218 yards
(100 grams, 199 meters) per skein]:
☐ Small amounts for **each** Flower

Crochet Hook
☐ Size E (3.25 mm)

Additional Supplies
☐ Yarn needle
☐ 1" (2.5 cm) wide Headband - 2
OR
☐ 2" (5 cm) Hair clip - 2
☐ Buttons/brads for flower
center

GAUGE INFORMATION
Gauge is not essential for this project.

INSTRUCTIONS
Flower #1
Finished Size: Our sample is 2¼"
(5.5 cm) across. Flower size will vary
depending on the type of yarn or
crochet cotton you use.

Skills Learned: This project will
help you practice your **Double
Crochets** (dcs).

Ch 52.

Row 1: Dc in 3rd ch from hook, 2 dc
in each ch across, ch 1, turn (100 dcs).

Row 2: Sl st in 1st dc, *ch 1, sl st in
next dc; rep from * across, ch 3 and
join with sl st to beg ch row. Fasten
off leaving a 20" (51 cm) tail.

Bottom Circle Cap
Work a Small Circle for the bottom
cap; see Circle instructions on
page 31.

Finishing
Thread a yarn needle with the 20"
(51 cm) tail, coil flower and secure in
place with a few whipstitches (see
photo below), making sure you stitch
through all thicknesses.

Attach button or brad to center of
flower. Place bottom circle cap on
bottom of flower, stitch circle cap to
flower with whipstitch. Hot Glue clip
to the bottom of the flower. You may
also use the flower on a headband;
see finishing instructions for Flower
#2, page 30.

Flower #2

Finished Size: Our sample is 4" (10 cm) across x 10" (25.5 cm) circumference. Flower size will vary depending on the type of yarn or crochet cotton you will use.

Skills Learned: This project will help you practice your **Double Crochets** (dcs) and **Half Double Crochets** (hdcs).

Ch 62.

Row 1: Dc in 3rd ch from hook, 2 dc in each ch across, ch 2, turn, (120 dcs).

Row 2: 2 Dc in each dc across to the last 10 dc, end with hdc in next 6 dc, sc in next 3 dc, sl st in last dc, ch 3 and join with sl st to beg ch row, (230 sts). Fasten off leaving a 20" (51 cm) tail.

Bottom Circle Cap

Work a Large Circle for the bottom cap; see Circle instructions on page 31.

Finishing

Thread a yarn needle with the 20" (51 cm) tail, coil flower and secure in place with a few whipstitches (see photo, page 28), making sure you stitch through all thicknesses.

Attach button or brad to center of flower.

Place Large Circle cap on bottom of flower; stitch circle cap to flower with whipstitch leaving two ½" (12 mm) openings to slip headband through.

Flower #3

Finished Size: Our sample is 4½" (11.5 cm) across x 10" (25.5 cm) circumference. Flower size will vary depending on the type of yarn or crochet cotton you will use.

Skills Learned: This project will help you practice your **Double Crochets** (dcs) and **Half Double Crochets** (hdc).

Ch 72.

Row 1: Dc in 3rd ch from hook, 2 dc in each ch across, ch 2, turn, (140 dcs).

Row 2: 2 Hdc in each dc across to last 4 dc, end with sc in next 3 dc, sl st in last dc, ch 1, turn, (276 sts).

Row 3: Sl st in 1st sc, *ch 1, sl st in next st; rep from * across, ch 3 and join with sl st to beg ch row. Fasten off leaving a 20" tail.

Bottom Circle Cap

Work a Large Circle for the bottom cap; see Circle instructions on page 31.

Finishing

Thread a yarn needle with the 20" (51 cm) tail, coil flower and secure in place with a few whipstitches (see photo, page 28), making sure you stitch through all thicknesses.

Attach button or brad to center of flower.

Place Large Circle cap on bottom of flower; stitch circle cap to flower with whipstitch leaving two ½" (12 mm) openings to slip headband through.

Small Circle

approximately 1¾" (4.5 cm) across

Skills Learned: Making a **Magic Ring** (see pg. 44) and practicing your **Single Crochets** (scs).

Make a Magic Ring.

Rnd 1: Ch 1, work 8 sc in ring. Join with sl st to beg sc, (8 sts).
Rnd 2: Ch 1, 2 sc in each sc. Join with sl st to beg sc, (16 sts).

Rnd 3: Ch 1, sc in each sc. Join with sl st to beg sc, (16 sts).

Rnd 4: Ch 1, sc in 1st sc, *2 sc in next sc, sc in next sc; rep from * around. Join with sl st to beg sc, (24 sts).

Rnds 5-6: Rep Rnd 3 until circle measures approximately 1¾" (4.5 cm) across. Join with sl st to beg sc.

Edging (optional)
Rnd 1: Sl st in 1st sc, *ch 1, sl st in next sc; rep from * across. Join with sl st to beg sl st. Fasten off. Weave in ends.

Medium Circle

approximately 2" (5 cm) across

Skills Learned: Making a **Magic Ring** (see pg. 44) and practicing your **Single Crochets** (scs).

Make a Magic Ring.

Rnds 1-4: Rep Rnds 1-4 of Small Circle. Join with sl st to beg sc, (24 sts).

Rnd 5: Ch 1, sc in 1st sc, *2 sc in next sc, sc in next 2 sc; rep from * around. Join with sl st to beg sc, (32 sts).

Rnds 6-7: Rep Rnd 3 until circle measures approximately 2" (5 cm) across. Work optional Edging instructions from Small Circle.

Large Circle

approximately 2¾" (7 cm) across

Skills Learned: Making a **Magic Ring** (see pg. 44) and practicing your **Single Crochets** (scs).

Make a Magic Ring.

Rnds 1-5: Rep Rnds 1-4 of Medium Circle. Join with sl st to beg sc, (32 sts).

Rnd 6: Ch 1, sc in 1st sc, *2 sc in next sc, sc in next 3 sc; rep from * around. Join with sl st to beg sc, (40 sts).

Rnds 7-8: Rep Rnd 3 until circle measures approximately 2¾" (7 cm) across. Work optional Edging instructions from Small Circle.

Cross Body Phone Sleeve

◼◼◻◻ **BEGINNER**

Finished Size: 3½" wide x 6½" height (9 cm x 16.5 cm)

SHOPPING LIST

Yarn (Light Weight)

[3.5 ounces, 218 yards
(100 grams, 199 meters) per skein]:

☐ 1 Skein

Thread (Size 5)

[27 yards (24.5 meters) per skein]:

☐ 2 **Each** color - (for Florets only)

Crochet Hooks

☐ Size E (3.5 mm)
   or size needed for gauge

☐ Steel, Size 4 (1.75 mm) for
   Florets only)

Additional Supplies

☐ Yarn needle

☐ Brads or Buttons for Floret
   center (optional)

☐ ⅛" (3 mm) Decorative Cord -
   52" long (132 cm)

GAUGE INFORMATION

5 sts = 1" (2.5 cm) 5 rows =1" (2.5 cm)

Even though gauge is not crucial for this project, you still want to make sure that you have the correct tension for the proper size; your phone might not fit in the case if you don't achieve the gauge. You can change hook size or yarn weight to correct your tension and achieve the right gauge.

Match your work to the graphic on page 35 to make sure you are on target for the right size.

INSTRUCTIONS

Skills Learned: Single crochets are the core of this lovely Phone Sleeve. You will also learn to make small florets that can be used in a variety of projects, from decorating headbands, a brooch, to using them for jewelry.

Main Section
Ch 17.

Rnd 1: 2 Sc in 2nd ch from hook, sc in next 14 scs, 3 sc in last ch, turn to work on the bottom loop of chain (see graph A), sc in next 14 sts, 1 sc in same ch as beg 2 sc. Join with sl st to beg sc, (34 sts).

Graph A

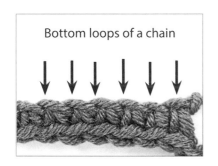
Bottom loops of a chain

Rnds 2-32: Ch 1, sc in 1st sc, sc in each sc around, (34 sts).

Do **not** fasten off.

Flap
Rnd 1: Ch 1, sc in 1st sc, sc in the next 16 scs, ch 1, turn, (17 sts).

Rnds 2-13: Ch 1, sc in 1st sc, sc in each sc across, ch 1, turn, (17 sts).

Rnd 14: Ch 1, *sl st in next sc, ch 1; rep from * 8 times, ch 5 for buttonhole, sk next sc, *sl st in next sc, ch 1; rep from * 8 times. Fasten off. Weave in ends.

Florets (make 5)
With Steel Hook 4/1.75mm and double strand of #5 thread, make a Magic Ring (see pg. 44).

Rnd 1: *Ch 2, 3 dc, sl st in ring; rep 4 more times to make a five petal floret, you can also make 3 or 4 petal florets depending on how many times you repeat the petals. Fasten off. Weave in ends.

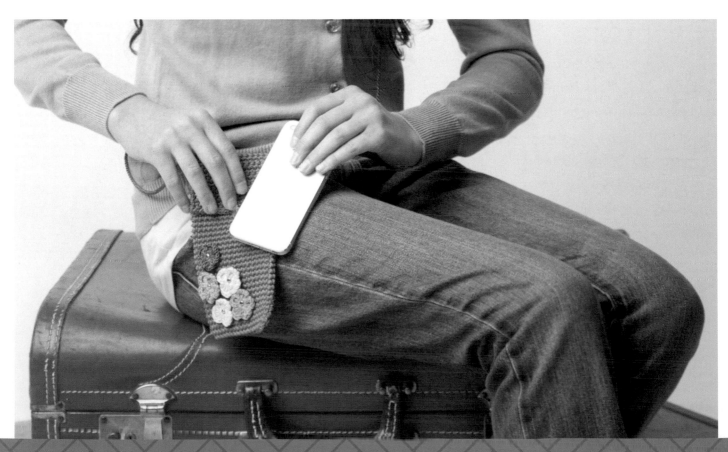

Finishing

Attach a brad to each floret center. With fabric glue, secure each floret to the Phone Sleeve. Mark placement for button and sew in place securely. Thread each end of the cord through the base of the flap on the sides, go from the outside in, and tie a knot at each end of cord to secure in place. If you are using a synthetic cord, have an adult melt end of cord with a lighter to keep it from fraying.

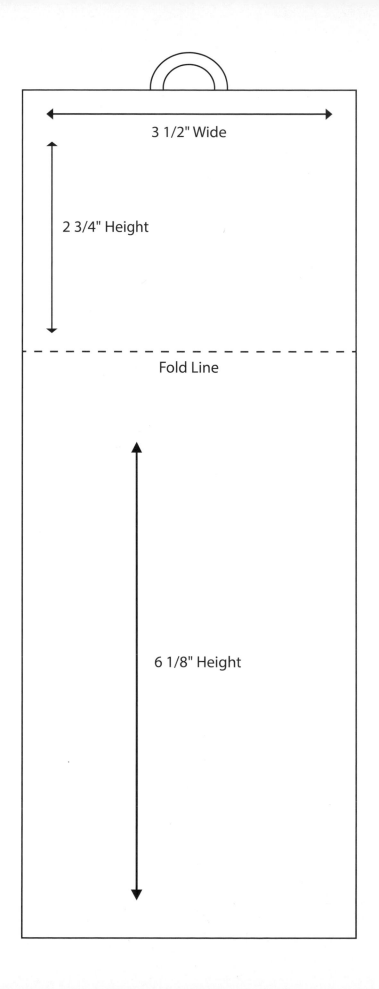

3 1/2" Wide

2 3/4" Height

Fold Line

6 1/8" Height

Neck Cuff to Hat

The Neck Cuff to Hat is worked with a chunky texture and a loose tension for a soft feel.

BEGINNER

Finished Size: 10" height x 21½" circumference (25.5 cm x 54.5 cm)

SHOPPING LIST

Yarn (Medium Weight) **4 MEDIUM**

[3.5 ounces, 220 yards
(100 grams, 201 meters) per skein]:

☐ 1 Skein

Crochet Hook

☐ Size G (4 mm)
or size needed for gauge

GAUGE INFORMATION

3 sts = 1" (2.5 cm), 3½ rows = 1" (2.5 cm)

Crochet a 12 ch 8 rows square swatch of scs to check your tension. Correct your tension if necessary to make sure you have the right gauge before you get started; you can change hook size or yarn weight to correct your tension and achieve the right gauge. You may use any yarn that will yield the gauge.

INSTRUCTIONS

Skills Learned: This project will help you learn how to work your **Single Crochets (scs)** in the **front loop** and in the **back loop** to achieve a soft and stretchy fabric texture.

Neck Cuff

Ch 60, join to beg ch being careful **not** to twist the chain.

Rnd 1: Ch 1, sc in 1st ch, sc in each ch around, (60 sts).

Rnd 2: Ch 1, sc in 1st sc, *sc in **front loop only** of next sc, sc in **back loop only** of next sc; rep from * around, end with sc in last sc. Join with sl st to beg sc, (60 sts).

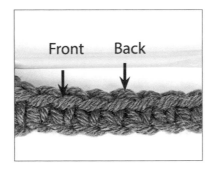

Front   Back

Rnds 3-28: Rep Rnd 2 until Cuff measures 10" (25.5 cm) or desired length, (60 sts).

Rnd 29: Ch 1, sc in each sc around, (60 sts).

Do **not** fasten off.

Top Edging (work in **front loops only**)

Rnd 1: Ch 1, sc in 1st sc, *ch 1, sl st in next sc; rep from * around. Join with sl st to beg sc. Fasten off. Weave in ends.

Bottom Edging (work in loops of beg chain)

Turn Neck Cuff upside down to work on the opposite end of Cuff and join yarn at beg of rnd.

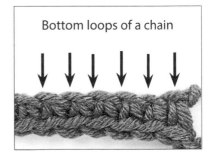

Bottom loops of a chain

Rnd 1: Rep Rnd 1 of Top Edging.

Finishing

Block Cuff, see pg. 47.

Boho Bag with Pom-poms

BEGINNER

Finished Size: 10½" height x 22" circumference (26.5 cm x 56 cm)

SHOPPING LIST

Thread (Size 10)

[350 yards (320 meters) per ball]:

☐ Coral - 2 balls

Size 5

[27 yards (24.5 meters) per skein]:

☐ 2 **Each** color - (for Florets only)

Crochet Hooks

☐ Size B/1 (2.25 mm)

or size needed for gauge

☐ Steel Size 4 (1.75 mm)

Additional Supplies

☐ Pom-pom maker (or see page 46)

Bag is worked holding two strands of thread together throughout.

GAUGE INFORMATION

6 sts = 1" (2.5 cm), 6 rows =1" (2.5 cm)

Gauge is not crucial for this project; however, try to stay within the requested gauge by measuring your project against the graphic measurements on page 41 when you make the bottom section.

About our Boho Bag:

The bag is made of a Bottom and a Body sections. As you crochet, make sure that you stay within the stitch count and measurement to ensure the best results. Pom-poms and Florets are optional; you may create your own dangling charms to personalize your bag!

INSTRUCTIONS

Skills Learned: With this project you will practice your **chains (chs)**, **slip stitches (sl sts)**, **single crochets (scs)**, and **double crochets (dcs)**. You will also learn to make small Florets that can be used in a variety of projects, from headbands to jewelry.

BOTTOM SECTION

With hook B/1-2.25mm and two strands of crochet cotton thread, make a Magic Ring (see pg. 44).

Rnd 1: Ch 1, 8 sc in ring. Join with sl st to beg sc, (8 sts).

Rnd 2: Ch 1, 2 sc in each sc around. Join with sl st to beg sc, (16 sts).

Rnd 3: Ch 1, sc in 1st sc, *2 sc in next sc, sc in next sc; rep from * around. Join with sl st to beg sc, (24 sts).

Rnd 4: Ch 1, *sc in next 2 sc, 2 sc in next sc; rep from * around. Join with sl st to beg sc, (32 sts).

Rnd 5: Ch 1, *sc in next 3 sc, 2 sc in next sc; rep from * around. Join with sl st to beg sc, (40 sts).

Rnd 6: Ch 1, *sc in next 4 sc, 2 sc in next sc; rep from * around. Join with sl st to beg sc, (48 sts).

Rnd 7: Ch 1, *sc in next 5 sc, 2 sc in next sc; rep from * around. Join with sl st to beg sc, (56 sts).

Rnd 8: Ch 1, *sc in next 6 sc, 2 sc in next sc; rep from * around. Join with sl st to beg sc, (64 sts).

Rnd 9: Ch 1, *sc in next 7 sc, 2 sc in next sc; rep from * around. Join with sl st to beg sc, (72 sts).

Rnd 10: Ch 1, *sc in next 8 sc, 2 sc in next sc; rep from * around. Join with sl st to beg sc, (80 sts).

Rnd 11: Ch 1, *sc in next 9 sc, 2 sc in next sc; rep from * around. Join with sl st to beg sc, (88 sts).

Rnd 12: Ch 1, *sc in next 10 sc, 2 sc in next sc; rep from * around. Join with sl st to beg sc, (96 sts).

Rnd 13: Ch 1, *sc in next 11 sc, 2 sc in next sc; rep from * around. Join with sl st to beg sc, (104 sts).

Rnd 14: Ch 1, *sc in next 12 sc, 2 sc in next sc; rep from * around. Join with sl st to beg sc, (112 sts).

You may add an extra round at this point if you want a bigger bag. Each round increases the size of the bag by 8 stitches or a little over an inch (2.5 cm).

BODY SECTION

Rnd 1: Ch 1, sc in 1st sc, *dc in next sc, sc in next sc; rep from * around. Join with sl st to beg sc, ch 1, turn, (112 sts).

Rnd 2: Dc in 1st sc, *sc in next dc, dc in next sc; rep from * around. Join with sl st to beg dc, ch 1, turn, (112 sts).

Rnds 3-26: Repeat Rnds 1 and 2 alternating. Join with sl st to beg st, on Rnd 26 don't ch 1 and turn, (112 sts).

Rnd 27: Ch 1, sc in 1st st, *ch 1, sk next st, sc in next st; rep from * around. Join with sl st to beg sc, ch 1, turn, (56 sts and 56 ch-1 spaces).

Rnd 28: Sc in 1st sc, *dc in next ch-1 space, sc in next sc; rep from * around. Join with sl st to beg sc, ch 1, turn, (112 sts).

Rnd 29: Dc in 1st sc, *sc in next dc, dc in next sc; rep from * around. Join with sl st to beg dc, ch 1, turn, (112 sts).

Rnds 30-33: Rep Rnds 28 and 29 alternating. Join with sl st to beg st, ch 1, turn, (112 sts).

EDGING

Rnd 1: Sc in 1st st, *ch 1, sc in next st; rep from * around. Join with sl st to beg sc. Fasten off. Weave in ends.

Cords (make 2)

With hook B/1-2.25mm, ch 151, sl st in 2nd ch from hook and in each ch across. Fasten off. Weave in ends.

Insert one of the cords through the ch spaces from Rnd 27, weave cord in and out skipping every other ch space all the way around, tie a knot to join ends. Starting on the opposite side of bag, repeat around with the second cord. Pull cords in opposite directions to close bag.

FLORETS

(optional, make 5 from colors of your choice)
With Steel hook 4/1.75mm and double strands of #5 thread, make a Magic Ring (see pg. 44).

Rnd 1: *Ch 2, 3 dc, sl st in ring; rep 4 times to make a five petal floret, or three times to make a three petal floret. Fasten off leaving a 8" tail.

Take the yarn tail and divide the strands in two groups, twist each group until strand starts to curl; pinch both groups at the top ends and tie a knot. The tail will twist together automatically. Trim ends.

POM-POMS

(make 3 from colors of your choice)
Make 3, 2" (5 cm) pom-poms using a pom-pom maker or see pg. 46 to make your own. Twist the yarn tails just like the Florets.

FINISHING

Gather all ends of the Florets and Pom-poms together, tie or pin together. Use a pin to attach to the center front of bag.

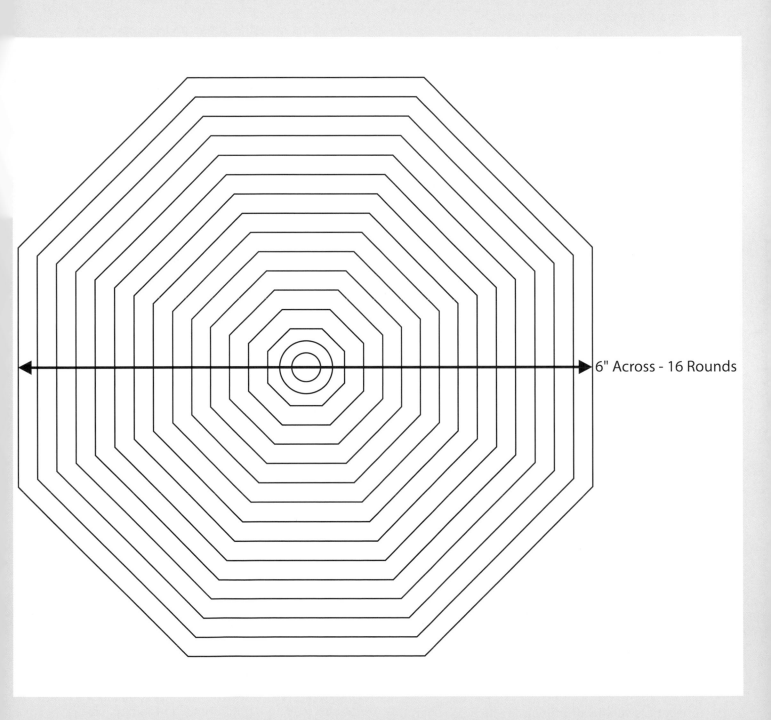

6" Across - 16 Rounds

Tension and Gauge

You can't have one without the other. Tension in crochet refers to how tight or loose you hold your yarn while you crochet. Gauge is the final size or fit of a garment you crochet or knit.

What you do with your tension will affect the gauge or fit of your project.

This is how it works, if you hold your yarn too tight, your stitches will be small and tight, sometimes so tight that you won't be able to put your hook through the next stitch! The result will be a tighter gauge or fit.

If you hold the yarn too loose, your stitches will be "loopy" and big and it will be confusing to see where the next stitch should be worked. The result will be a bigger gauge or fit.

It is important that you control your tension so it's not too tight, or too loose, but just right! Just like a sewing machine has knobs to control the thread tension, your left hand is crucial to control the tension and feed the yarn smoothly to the hook!

Your crochet projects will have a professional finish once you learn to master the tension. Just like a sewing machine has knobs to control the thread tension, your left hand is crucial to control the tension and feed the yarn smoothly to the hook.

What can you do to achieve the right tension? Try the following 4 steps to achieve the right tension or gauge.

Before you start a pattern, read what the Gauge is supposed to be for that specific pattern. Checking the Gauge is simply measuring the number of stitches and rows per inch of crocheting. Our patterns will specify how many stitches or rows you should get per inch; gauge is usually tested on a single crochet swatch.

1. To achieve the right tension and gauge you must start with the yarn and hook size specified in the pattern; you can choose a different yarn as long as it's the same weight as your pattern.

2. Crochet a swatch with the basic stitch specified in the pattern, usually a 2" x 2" or 4" x 4" swatch made of single crochets.

3. Block the swatch (see page 47) to help the yarn relax. Don't block acrylic yarns.

4. Place a ruler or a measuring tape across the center of swatch to see how many stitches "fit" in one inch. Do the same with the rows.

Some yarns have the gauge on the packaging; for example, you might see a grid, with a 16 on one side and an 18 on the other side and a hook with a number by it. This is very helpful as it tells you that the average crocheter using the hook size they specified will crochet a swatch measuring the same as the grid on the label.

Oh no! My gauge is not correct, what can I do? Try one or all of these 3 solutions to correct your gauge:
1. Try changing hook sizes, either a bigger hook for bigger stitches or a smaller hook for smaller stitches. 2. You may change yarn size and brand. 3. Hold your yarn tighter or loosen your grip on the yarn to adjust the tension. Check your gauge periodically to make sure your garment will be the right size when you're finished.

Why Gauge is Important
You want to have your gauge be as close as possible to the gauge the designer used; this will ensure that your garment will turn out approximately the same size as the pattern indicates. Note that we said approximately because every one crochets with a different tension which will cause a slight variation in size.

It's important to check your gauge before you start a project and see how your crocheting compares to the gauge of the pattern; you do this by working a small swatch.

Why Check Gauge?
Many crocheters think that working a swatch is a waste of time; however, you don't want to work forty hours on a garment that won't fit - that would be a bigger waste of time!

Gauge is important depending on the project. If you are making a scarf, a baby blanket, an afghan, flowers or a pillow, gauge might not matter much; but if you are working on a fitted project such as a hat or a garment, gauge makes a big difference. One little stitch per inch more or less can make a big difference in the final size of your project. With a little math you can figure how one stitch can make your project a couple of inches bigger or smaller.

Remember, change the hook, change the yarn, adjust the tension, and try again!

Stitch Guide

Holding the hook

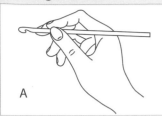

Holding the yarn

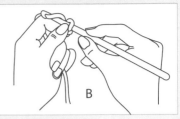

Slip knot

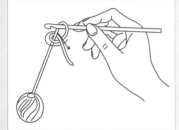

Start with a slip knot on your hook.

Yarn over (yo)

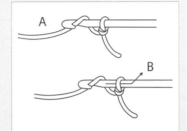

Yarn over (yo), pull through loop (lp) on hook.

Chain (ch)

Yarn over (yo), pull through loop (lp) on hook.

Slip stitch (sl st)

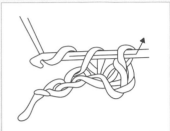

Insert hook in stitch (st), pull through both lps on hook.

Single crochet (sc)

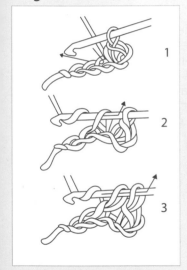

Insert hook in st, yo, pull through st, yo, pull through both lps on hook.

Half double crochet (hdc)

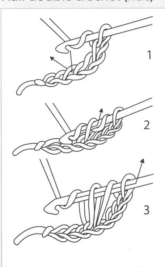

Yo, insert hook in st, yo, pull through st, yo, pull through all 3 lps on hook.

Double crochet (dc)

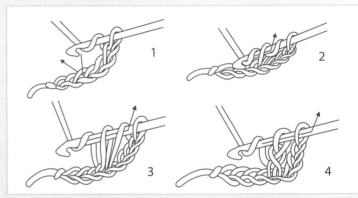

Yo, insert hook in st, yo, pull through st, [yo, pull through 2 lps] twice.

Treble crochet (tr)

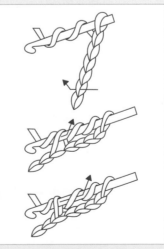

Yo twice, insert hook in st, yo, pull through st, [yo, pull through 2 lps] 3 times.

Double treble crochet (dtr)

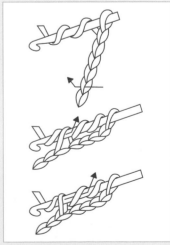

Yo 3 times, insert hook in st, yo, pull through st, [yo, pull through 2 lps] 4 times.

Front/back loop (front lp/back lp)

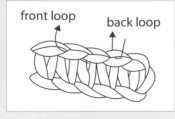

Changing colors

To change colors, drop the first color. With the second color, pull through last lp of st.

Stitch Guide

Magic Ring

A magic ring, also known as an adjustable ring or magic circle loop, is a starting technique for crocheting in rounds by creating a loop that allows you to put the stitches in; you can then draw the loop up tight to leave no visible hole in the center.

1 Leaving a 10" (25.5 cm) tail, wind the yarn from the yarn ball around your fingers as shown.

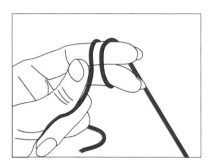

2 Grasp the yarn at the top where the strands overlap.

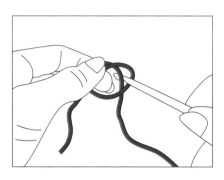

3 Insert the hook through the front of the ring and grab the yarn.

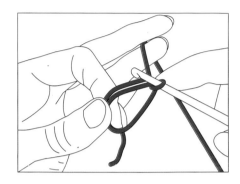

4 Pull up a loop.

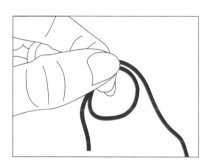

5 Chain 1; this chain is to "lock" the magic ring, it is not part of your stitch count. You may pull on the yarn to tighten the lock.

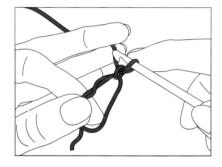

6 Chain 1, *insert hook through ring, yarn over, and pull through both loops on hook * (single crochet made); repeat from * to * to make as many single crochets as the pattern requires.

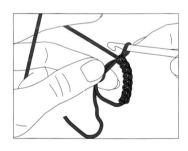

7 After completing the number of stitches in the ring, grab the tail and pull firmly to close the ring.

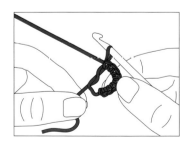

8 Join the ring with slip stitch by inserting hook through both loops of beginning single crochet (see pink arrow); don't insert hook through beginning "lock" stitch. Pull the tail again tightly to close center completely.

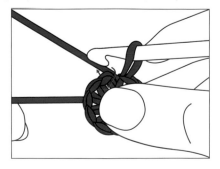

How to Make a Tassel

Cut a piece of cardboard the size of one of your credit cards, 2" x 3½" (5 cm x 9 cm).

1 Cut a piece of yarn 8 yards (7.5 meters) long and wrap around card lengthwise; you may use two different colors of yarn for each tassel (4 yards {3.5 meters} of each color).

2 Cut another piece of yarn 1 yard (1 meter) long and fold in half, slip through the middle of the wrapped yarn on one end of cardboard.

3 Tie a tight knot twice to hold tassel top together.

4 While holding the card, twist each group of strands at the top until they are tightly wound, making sure you twist each group in the same direction.

5 Pinch and hold both twisted ends together at the top and let go of the card, they will self twist together, tie ends together with a knot to secure in place and trim off uneven ends.

tie ends together with a knot

6 Slide tassel off the card and smooth down the loops.

7 Cut another piece of yarn 1 yard (1 meter) long and fold in half, wrap 5-6 times around tassel about ½" (12 mm) below the top, making sure you wrap it tight to keep tassel from becoming undone, tie a knot to secure in place.

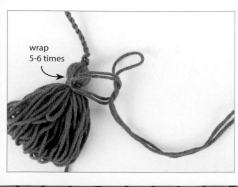

wrap 5-6 times

8 Cut bottom loops and trim off bottom of tassel evenly.

9 Thread the remaining tails from Step 7 through a yarn needle and weave in down through the center of tassel. Block if necessary (see page 47).

How to Make a Pom-pom

1 Cut 2 cardboard circles using pom-pom template on page 47. Cut a 36" (91.5 cm) piece of yarn, fold in half, and place between the two cardboard circles as shown below. Start wrapping yarn around the cardboard circles.

2 Wrap enough yarn around cardboard circles to make pom-pom thick and plump; with small sharp scissors, insert scissors between cardboard circles and cut yarn along the edge.

3 Cut along the edge being careful to keep pieces of yarn from falling off the cardboard.

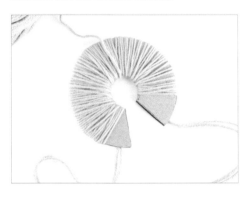

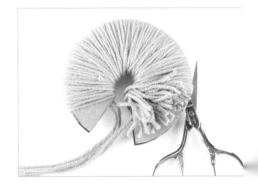

4 Tie a double knot with the 36" (91.5 cm) strand, making sure it's very tight. Move strands around opposite side of first knot and tie another double knot.

5 Remove cardboard circles and fluff pom-pom.

6 Take both ties and twist each in the same direction, wind each end until twist is tight, pinch both ends together and let go, both ends will self wind to form the cord. Tie ends with a knot.

7 Trim pom-pom all the way around to even all ends.

Completed Pom-pom
TIP: try using different colors of yarn on the same pom-pom for a fun look!

Running Stitch

Running stitch is a basic embroidery stitch we use often to attach embellishments. It is made by passing the needle through and bringing it out again.

Finishing Your Project

Blocking

Always check the yarn label for any special care instructions. Many natural fibers, such as cotton, linen, and wool, respond well to steam blocking. However, you shouldn't use steam or heat on mohair or angora. Many acrylics and some blends shouldn't be steamed blocked at all because they will not "bounce" back to show the stitch definition again, and they can also melt!

Use a hand towel or handkerchief and a padded ironing board. If you prefer, you can substitute a table or any flat surface that you have padded adequately.

Take the dampened towel or handkerchief, place it over the edge of the project, and steam with an iron, holding the iron slightly above the finished project. Lift the towel and repeat with another section all the way around. Leave the project in place until it is dry.

Pom-Pom Templates

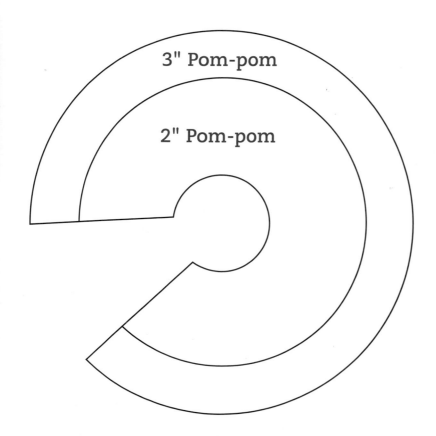

3" Pom-pom

2" Pom-pom

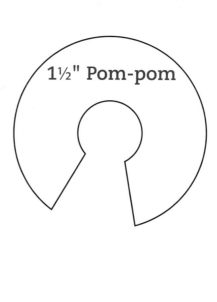

1½" Pom-pom

Yarn Information

For your convenience, listed below are the specific yarn styles and colors used to create our photography models. Because yarn manufacturers make frequent changes in their product lines, you may sometimes find it necessary to use a substitute yarn or to search for the discontinued product at alternate suppliers (locally or online).

Chain, Chain, Chain Necklace
Lion Brand® Bonbons
#601-650 Party

Bows on Clips
Omega® Sinfonia
#806114 Coral
#839185 Cream
#909107 Turquoise

Circle Me Pretty Necklace
Lion Brand® Bonbons
#601-650 Party

Flower Power
Omega® Sinfonia
#707507 Dark Magenta
#806114 Coral
#839786 Gold

Cross Body Phone Sleeve
Omega® Sinfonia #806114 Coral
Florets
DMC® Perle Cotton, size 5
#783, #209, #747, #712, #453

Neck Cuff to Hat
Cascade Yarns® 220 Superwash®
#900 Charcoal

Boho Bag with Pom-poms
Aunt Lydia's® Crochet Cotton, size 10
#275 Coral
Florets
DMC® Perle Cotton, size 5
#783, #209, #747, #712, #453